Dear Me

Dear Me

A Christian's Journal
Through Insecurity

Peter Stephens

Slow press

Bluemont, Virginia

Published by Slow Press
P. O. Box 92, Bluemont, Virginia 20135

SlowPress.com

ISBN 0-9758648-0-7

Printed in the United States of America.

To Michael Gress, Larry Kennedy, and Victoria

Thanks

"It is not we who choose to awaken ourselves, but God Who chooses to awaken us."

~ Thomas Merton,
New Seeds of Contemplation

Contents

Acknowledgements

My thanks to Betty Whitworth, who edited this into a much better book.

I am grateful to my wife, Victoria, for sharing her life in these pages. She also put up with my working late nights on yet another project.

Introduction

I have struggled with feelings of inadequacy most of my adult life. I wrote this book at age forty as a gift to myself, because my lack of self-confidence had become anguishing and debilitating. The completed book guided me to recovery.

Self-confidence seemed like a foundation that was never laid in me. As a young man, I often doubted my ability to take on new challenges, whether the challenges involved school, work, or personal relationships. I refused an offer to become the editor of my law school's newspaper because I judged myself inadequate for the job. After graduating, I was so nervous as a public speaker that perspiration often soaked my shirt. And I was a trial lawyer!

My insecurity hurt my social life, too. Well into my twenties I avoided most eligible, attractive woman. In the presence of an attractive woman, my awkwardness and constant swallowing telegraphed my anxiety and made the other person uncomfortable.

Things slowly improved. During my thirties I began to feel more and more at home in my small church fellowship. I found that I could share my struggles with some church members and receive support. With this new freedom and safety I felt in my church home, I became more at home with myself. I gained enough confidence to become a partner in our small law firm, and I became confident enough with women to (eventually) marry one!

Despite these successes, I knew that I remained fundamentally an insecure person. I thought I would continue to become a more confident person in the same way I had in the past: I would meet new challenges with the help of God and my church family.

That is not exactly what happened. I faced two new challenges as I approached my forties, and no amount of prayer or Bible study helped me overcome them. The first challenge involved a career change, and the second, ironically, involved my wife Victoria's own personal growth. These two challenges led directly to a mental and spiritual crisis.

The career change fulfilled a twenty-year desire. I stopped practicing law and became the associate pastor of my church in my late thirties. During my earlier years as a lawyer, I thought I was more secure than to define myself by my work. In fact, I thought I would be able to walk away from my law practice without any internal struggle. Instead, gnawing insecurity plagued me the first few years of pastoring. I felt disconnected from myself without my law practice.

In contrast to the long smoldering anxiety I experienced over the career change, my second challenge seemed like an unexpected volcanic eruption. In Victoria's process of becoming more secure in herself, she suddenly became much more expressive to me sexually. My response shocked me. Anxiety filled me and I retreated from her sexually, just as I had run away from women socially as a young man. Victoria could not enjoy her new sexual freedom.

To help improve our sex life, I went to see Dr. Larry Kennedy, a professional counselor. Dr. Kennedy pointed out that the challenges relating to my work and sex life were symptoms of my deep-seated insecurity. I had a choice: address only the symptoms or allow the symptoms to lead me to the roots of the insecurity.

For the first time in my life, I looked beneath the manifestation *de jour* of my insecurity and examined the insecurity itself. My commitment to this examination led directly to the crisis I had been avoiding for years. In a sense, then, the upcoming crisis turned out to be my decision.

At the urging of Dr. Kennedy and my pastor, Michael Gress, I began to identify and give up the false ideas I had unwittingly developed about myself to cover my insecurity. God gave me the grace to see the self-centered and sometimes self-contradictory lies I had assembled to create the way I thought about myself. "I'm a fearful person." "I'm a good Christian." "I'm a failure at life." "I'm better than others."

At that point the crisis came. In giving up these notions about myself, I discovered that I had no real sense of who I was. My insecurity became anguishing. I felt as if I was walking along the edge of a widening abyss that threatened to keep me lost to myself forever.

My wife, pastors, and counselor loved me and helped me through the struggle. Their love touched me, but nothing outside myself could cover the abyss I felt inside.

Simple things triggered anxiety. A trip to the post office to mail packages for the church filled me with fear. The trip reminded me that I was no longer a lawyer, no longer "myself." If Victoria did not wish to be intimate on occasion, I incorrectly took it as reflection on me. Most of the anxiety, though, was disconnected from outside events. A steady fear radiated from the emptiness I found inside. The only thing I found I knew about myself was that I was scared.

The struggle went on for a year, more or less. I functioned through it feeling less than a person. I thought I was masquerading as a husband, a father, and a pastor. An insecure child inside me seemed to be pulling the levers operating my hands, feet, and mouth, doing its best to act like an adult. I felt like a shell of a man.

The first few months of my crisis, I rarely slept more than two or three hours. I spent most of those nights in anguish, struggling to believe simple concepts I learned long ago, such as God's love for me. I prayed, I cried, but mostly I stayed awake and waited for sleep. I know now that God was answering some of my oldest prayers, my simplest prayers of devotion: "Bring me close to you, Lord." "Purify me, Lord." "Lord, have mercy." And, "Jesus."

During those nights I also read. At Dr. Kennedy's recommendation I began to read a lot of devotional classics. I discovered struggles and truths that I could relate to in the writings of Augustine, Søren Kierkegaard, Henri Nouwen and others. Their books have become like old friends.

I kept a journal from the outset of my crisis. It included perceived advances and setbacks, advice and descriptions of truths that struck me as important, and realizations that came during work or on walks.

One sleepless night I decided to summarize some of the contents of my journal, so I would have its encouragement in a more accessible form. I wrote most of this book that night. The new book quickly became my primary devotional. Its directives summarized the truths I was learning in a way that spoke directly to my soul.

Months passed and I began to believe the things I wrote in this book. Like a coffeepot, I allowed the book's truths to drip down from my head into my heart. I began to see that I was deeply loved. The anxiety I once felt when I was alone, at work, or in bed with my wife, slowly diminished. Sleep returned to normal. The crisis ebbed, but I still read this book as a means of correcting my thinking and getting back on course when necessary.

Publishing the book at the time I wrote it would have embarrassed me and slowed my recovery. I put the idea out of my mind for a few years. My discretion benefited my recovery, so that now I can make my crisis available to others without fear of a reversal.

I have tried to keep the book personal by retaining the second person voice I used to speak to myself. I have retained most references to personal problems and personal revelation in order to be faithful to the book's essence: a personal journal. I hope the cumulative effect of these references encourages some others to write the truths they are learning in a way that they can readily hear from themselves.

One personal phenomenon I should address is the "images" I refer to in the book. These are mental pictures that summarize a truth for me better than words. I credit God with these pictures. They come from outside myself. These images, or "visions" as some people dare to label them, are not uncommon experiences for many Christians.

The book generally follows the chronological order of the crisis, from Dr. Kennedy's initial challenge ("The Joy is in the Journey," for instance), to my despair ("Use Your Sin and Shame"), to new hope ("Let Hope Come"), to repentance for specific sin patterns ("Don't Shift Blame"). As my despair turned to hope, I found I was prepared to address the sin I found bundled with my insecurity.

The directives need not be read in the order presented, however. The table of contents may help the reader find insights or disciplines that benefit his or her own situation.

Dear Me

The Joy is in the Journey

Your lack of self-confidence comes from the distance you put between your family and yourself as a teenager. You rejected the identity your family offered, and you came up with your own identity, which was based on judgments against your family and yourself. Consequently, most of the identity you claim is not true.

You will find who you are as result of a spiritual journey. The joy is not in arriving at some destination. The joy is in the journey! The journey is a process and not a list of things to accomplish.

[Ephesians 4:20-24]

Feed the Authentic You

Your "authentic" self is well defined, but you can't define it, because it is unknown to you. It is like a baby presently. You must feed it and take care of it, and it will grow. Feed "self" with God's thoughts. This nourishment will help you walk in God's love.

[2 Corinthians 4:16; Galatians 4:19; Colossians 3:10; Jude 20-21]

Your Identity is in Another

Your identity is not in your abilities or disabilities. Your identity is in the thoughts Jesus had about you when he walked with the cross to his death. By God's choice, you are worth the death of his Son. From this center, your thoughts and actions will become responses to Jesus' love.

[Jeremiah 31:3]

Learn to Keep Your Eyes on Jesus

You feel like God has put you in a grave and that something rotten inside of you is slowly disintegrating.

Choose to set the Lord before you continually. Comfort yourself with Jesus' death and resurrection! Take communion with others and by yourself. Use your imagination. See Jesus very close to you. This will help your flesh "dwell securely" in the grave, or "rest in hope" as the King James Version states it.

[Psalm 16]

Your Death is Your Family's Inheritance

You are concerned that people who depend on you will suffer because, during this difficult time, you are not functioning as well as you have in the past. But the best gift you can give them is your willingness to go through a "death" experience to your sin nature. By God's grace, your children will not inherit your sin.

[Numbers 14:30-31]

Rejoice in God's Provision

Your soul is in a desert, but even the desert has flowers. You have become thankful for small graces you would not have noticed before this desert walk ~ a friend's phone call, a breeze, a sweet recollection, a quiet room with a good book. God's provision for you in the desert teaches you to abide in God alone and to trust in him. It takes a long struggle to teach this. Note God's provisions as milestones and as tokens of Jesus' affection.

[Deuteronomy 8:3 & 32:7-14]

All the Old Truths Apply

Continue in the Bible's truths you have learned over the years. They still apply to you. You will receive fresh revelation as you apply the old truths to your current struggles.

[Philippians 3:16]

Walk Through it for Jesus' Sake

You must walk through the crisis for Jesus ~ not for yourself. The crisis is not primarily for your healing, though your healing will come. It is not for your wife or even for your children, though they will benefit. Your crisis is for Jesus only. He alone makes the pain worthwhile!

You had a mental image of God in a storage room looking for a vessel. He found you in the corner, piled up with a lot of other stuff, and you were covered with moss and grime. God said, "How about this one? He has always wanted me to use him." And he began the job of cleaning you for his service. You became thankful.

This is the purpose of your
suffering and the source of your joy.

[2 Corinthians 4:11]

Own Your Poop

A year before the crisis, you had a mental image in which you were alone on a hill, happy in the darkness. As the sun began to rise, you noticed more and more poop on the ground around you. The ground was covered! Dawn also revealed Jesus standing beside you, nodding. "Yeah. That's your poop."

Jesus insists that you own your sin. Never be shocked by Jesus' point of view concerning your sin. Take Jesus' point of view as your own and rely on his sacrifice and love instead of your own righteousness. By doing this over and over, you train your eyes to adjust to the light, and you begin to see your sin ~ and yourself ~ as Jesus does.

[Jeremiah 3:12-13]

Become Radically Dependent

Stop approaching sin with the idea you can resist it. Otherwise, God will resist you. He gives grace to the humble, though. The best place to be during the storms of temptation is in the hold of humility.

When you are tempted, immediately admit you are powerless and ask for God's mercy and grace. You are completely dependent on God's mercy.

[James 4:6-10]

Use Your Sin and Shame

"I am a sinner, Lord, and you love me despite my sin."

Let occurrences of sin and shame become occasions for God to show you how much he loves you. The sin and shame will cause you to wash Jesus' feet with tears and wipe them with your hair. Thus, the memory of the sin and shame will become bittersweet with time.

[Luke 7:36-50]

Watch God Fix It

Do not run from your problems nor grovel in them! Neither of these extremes works. Instead, bring the problems to God. Give him time, and watch him fix them.

[Psalm 40:1-2 & 41:4]

Settle God's Ability and Willingness to Heal You

You sometimes doubt God's ability or his willingness to heal you. Settle this issue! Your healing is part of Christ's redemption. God will heal you in his way and in his time.

[Matthew 8:2-3]

Smash Every Clock

Setting an expected time of healing is like setting an alarm clock. You place many alarm clocks along your pathway to wholeness. You place some at perceived milestones, and others at certain points in the recurring "cycle" of your feelings. When you reach one of these points, an alarm clock rings, and you feel you should have made more progress than you recognize. Smash the clock each time! Your times are God's business alone ~ not yours. "My times are in Your hand," David wrote.

[Psalm 31:14-15]

Discover Patience

Joy is the last thing you feel in the midst of a trial or temptation. But Paul and James say you can be joyful because trials and temptations produce patience. This does not make you joyful, though, because you see no need for patience.

The main purpose of patience is to steady and strengthen your desire to be with Jesus forever. Patience, Paul says, gives space for character development, and proven character leads to real hope. You have no use for patience, because your hope is not in the next life yet.

Take God's eternal perspective. This will help you be patient with God and yourself.

[Romans 5:3-5; James 1:2-4 & 5:7-8]

Be Content with Weakness

To be joyful in temptation requires a celebration of your humanity. You must remain your own friend even in all your weakness.

Use your weakness to the max. Where you are poor in spirit, you will have Jesus who made himself poor for us. Paul learned to be content in every circumstance, and he was "well content with weakness."

[James 1:2-4; 2 Corinthians 8:9; 12:10 & 13:4; Philippians 4:11]

Be as Happy as God

When you cried out to God about your problems, you took his Spirit to say, "Are things hard for you? Things are fine where I am." You are called to be where Jesus is! If things are fine with God, things should be fine with you, no matter what the circumstances or perplexities.

If God chooses not to deliver you for a long time, you can be just as happy as if he delivered you quickly. That is because your Master is happy. If Jesus is happy, be happy!

[Psalm 91]

Let Hope Come

You want to hit the golf ball straight and far. But if you concentrate on hitting the ball, you will shank it. The key is to follow through ~ to concentrate on what happens after the ball is hit. Absurdly, what happens after the ball is hit affects how the ball is hit.

Hope in eternal life is like follow-through. The future affects the present. If you allow God to develop in you the hope of Jesus' return, you will shoot a better game in this life. Your beloved's return is the best motivation for purifying yourself, and purification leads to true happiness in this life. Of course, a better life here will not be as important as before, since your hope is in the next life.

If your interest is in only your character and its improvement, you are still focused on hitting the ball.

[1 John 3:2-3]

You Are Hidden

Every important event either happened before you were born or will happen after you are dead. Before you ever had a chance to mess up, Jesus thought of you as he walked to his death. He died for you. After you die, Jesus will return and bring your life back with him. In the meantime, you have given Jesus your life as a reasonable response to his love for you. You do not have a life anymore; your life is hidden with Christ in God.

[Colossians 3:1-4; Galatians 2:20]

You Have No Rights

You tend to desire anything you find attractive. You are possessive of Victoria because of this, and because you have experienced love from her. But God alone is the source of all love, even the love Victoria has shown you. You must give up possession of Victoria if you want your relationship to bloom.

Since your life is not your own, you do not have any rights. Stop looking to be satisfied in this life outside of God. Only God can satisfy you. When he satisfies you, he makes you hungry for the next life. This hunger brings a sharper perspective.

Jesus gave up all his rights. To follow Jesus, you must stop insisting on what you think are your rights. You have no right to sex. Sex is a gift. Life itself is a gift.

Oswald Chambers has it right. As you give up your right to yourself, perplexing problems become balls of knots you can enjoy watching God unravel!

[Psalm 17:14-15; I Corinthians 6:19-20]

See Yourself as Apprehended

You cannot stop feeling possessive of others if you do not have a deep sense of belonging. Work with God to develop this part of your relationship with him. See yourself as Benjamin, the object of his father's love. The Bible is silent about Benjamin's accomplishments, but his father loved him anyway.   Remember Moses' blessing for Benjamin: "The beloved of the Lord!" Take it as your own.

[I Corinthians 3:21-23; Deuteronomy 33:12]

Your Loneliness is a Gift

In this struggle, you have discovered that you are lonely. Only God can meet that loneliness. Do not despise your loneliness; see it as a gift from God for him to fill, like a beautiful cup.

[Isaiah 61:1-3]

Jesus is Your Beloved

You have put a great burden on Victoria and your marriage by insisting that Victoria meet your emotional needs. Victoria was not designed to meet your emotional needs. Jesus will meet them, though. Treat him as your fiancé.

[2 Corinthians 11:2; Revelation 19:7-9]

Make Friends, Work Hard, and Write Often

Work hard. That will keep your mind off yourself during this struggle. Develop friendships. That will take away some of the undue pressure you have put on your wife. Read and write. That will enhance your relationship with God and help you gain clarity about what you are going through.

[Proverbs 17:17]

Choose to See God in Everyday Life

Nature and small daily events remind you of God's love or of some important lesson, if you let them.

Choose to see God in summer rain, in a flower on a path, or in a poem etched onto the floor of a gazebo. Accepting these kinds of gifts is like accepting the "still small voice" you hear on occasion.

Choose to receive God's love spoken softly, and you heart will become tender.

[I Kings 19:11-12]

Remember Jesus' Eyes

The morning of your wedding, you sensed the Holy Spirit's grief. You knew your fellowship with God would suffer from the marriage. That does not mean it was a mistake to marry. It means you were fixed on substituting Victoria for God. God is using this struggle to restore Jesus' place as your beloved and to put your marriage in its proper place.

Three years ago, God showed you a powerful image of Jesus looking at you with the eyes of a lover. His expression was engaging and jealous, like a lover's. You felt both broken and happy, because you thought your marriage had ended a close relationship with Jesus.

A moment later, God allowed you to see yourself as a furnace. As the fire burned, light from the furnace flashed different colors. The colors represented impurities God wanted to burn out of your life.

Both of these images are beginning to be fulfilled. The purpose of this struggle is to remove impurities, but the greater purpose is to prepare you for your beloved Jesus. Victoria has beautiful eyes, but you have never seen eyes like Jesus' eyes, and you never will in this life. Let the longing come.

[Song of Solomon 5:12; Isaiah 48:10]

Return to the Quiet Space

You have practiced quiet *times*, but the quiet was external. In your quiet time, your mind still raced and you resisted quietness, although you did not wish to resist.

God is developing a quiet *space* in you for the two of you to share. Some sort of invisible portal leads to this space. If you neglect this space, you will lose your feel for its portal.

This space is so holy to you. Be silent about it.

[Matthew 6:6; Psalm 91:1]

Get Paid for Being Alive

Your legal work launched you toward self-worth. That happened because you did not seek your self-worth from more appropriate places. Now what? You can no longer rely on your legal work to meet that need.

So much of your new work as an associate pastor seems trivial compared to legal work. You realize the mundane part of your new work is for a season, but fear still grips you as you perform "menial" tasks. This fear comes from the old way you defined your identity. Repent of the underlying arrogance that places your point of view above God's. You do not have to be miserable.

You recognize "unproductive" times on the job. Sometimes

circumstances arrange themselves to hinder production. During these times, you must simply be. When fear accompanies these unproductive times, repent of the same arrogance.

God does not desire you to draw your identity from your job. He is helping you deal with this issue through the new job. Remember what Victoria said: "Peter, sometimes I think God is paying you just to be alive."

God wants to be the source of your identity. Let God express with his dollars what he wants you to know in your heart. You are worth everything to him. Your performance is not.

[Romans 5:8-10; Titus 3:4-7]

Lose the Win-Lose Paradigm

You think the inability to do something produces much of the fear you feel. However, inability produces frustration, not fear. You experience fear when you are unable to accomplish a task, because you think others will see you as a failure.

Your fears are groundless. In fact, you are the harshest critic you have. Since you are God's and not your own, your self-criticism amounts to arrogance.

In your eyes, life amounts to either success or failure. Relax! Give yourself permission to enjoy the moment. Move out of the win-lose metaphor of life.

[Romans 14:4]

Enjoy the Free Fall

You must move from your old, familiar habits and thinking to God's habits and thinking. You have to depend on God to move like that, but your fear keeps you from dependence. You are afraid you will lose control of your life's outcome.

Do not place your trust in a particular outcome but in God and his faithfulness. This kind of trust can be compared to falling off a cliff backward and knowing God's hands will catch you. Do not grasp for branches on the way down in an effort to slow the fall. Go ahead and achieve terminal velocity. As you achieve this, you lose your control. You lose your expectations as well as other things that serve to hold you back.

[Matthew 21:44; Isaiah 35:8]

God is in the Darkness

You feel discouraged because the truth you received from God and your counselors has not stemmed the fear or humiliation. The thoughts behind these feelings are not always apparent. Your applications of the truth against these feelings appear hopeless, like efforts to reverse the incoming tide.

Do not be upset with God, the counselors or yourself. Rely on the truth God has shown you, even if that truth appears incomplete.

Do not create your own light. Walk in darkness and trust in God. The way to God is through darkness.

[Isaiah 50:10-11; Psalm 18:11;
Psalm 97:2]

Thoughts Cause Feelings

Fear and humiliation engender more fear and humiliation. Identify the thoughts behind these feelings, and you will begin to break this unpleasant cycle.

Feelings are merely symptoms of thoughts. Trying to change your feelings is like trying to change medical symptoms while ignoring their source. As long as the source is there, the symptoms will recur! Instead, identify the thoughts that cause unpleasant feelings. Then, put God's thoughts in your mind to eradicate your cancerous thoughts.

Do not be concerned if the feelings linger a long time. Address the thoughts, and the feelings will eventually depart.

You tend to measure your progress by your feelings. When fear returns, for instance, you feel discouraged and think you are losing the fight. Remember, fears are only symptoms. If you choose to believe God's love in the midst of your struggles and fears, you win! The fears indicate the battleground. They do not indicate who wins.

[Judges 6 & 7; I John 4:16]

Your Behavior is Still Important

Your feelings of humiliation sometimes combine with frustration and tempt you to express yourself inappropriately. These temptations disturb you, because you have not experienced them in a long time.

You cannot evaluate your progress by your temptations. Otherwise, you will lose heart and give in to temptations, which would make things worse.

Remember to behave yourself. Love does not act unbecomingly.

[I Corinthians 13:4-5]

Close the Escape Hatches

You are on a journey to your true center, which is your more authentic self. Lifelong habits have become means of escape from this journey. You must close these escape hatches in order to realize your true self. If things are not right, you should suspect one or more opened hatches. These hatches must be closed over and over before they remain closed permanently.

Ask God to continue exposing your engrained thinking, which is contrary to his thinking. Pray for mercy as he exposes this type of thinking.

[Galatians 6:14]

Don't Shift Blame

Blame shifting is an escape from your journey to authenticity. You want to blame Victoria for not helping more with your insecurity. Face the truth. You know where this thinking is heading; you want to make Victoria responsible for your insecurity.

Your sin is you own. Pause and consider how sensitive and loving Victoria has been to you during your crisis, despite the burden it has placed on her. Remember, your healing does not depend on Victoria!

[Genesis 3:11-13]

Discover Your Willfulness

Your feelings of self-pity stem from a belief that you can't do God's will. When you think you can't, you are being willful, since God says you can. "I can't" really means "I won't." Admit your willfulness to yourself and to God.

[Luke 22:41-42]

Become Conscious of Your Passive-Aggressive Behavior

You act like a little boy when you acquiesce in Victoria's decisions, and then you silently get her back later. Instead of this passive aggression, be simple and forthcoming with Victoria about your feelings and thoughts. In addition, let Victoria show you when you may be operating in your passive-aggressive pattern. This will take practice and humility.

[I Kings 21:1-6]

Surrender Your Should's and Ought's

When Victoria makes you angry, be conscious of your feelings that she "shouldn't" act the way she does. Remember that our thoughts lead to our actions. Based on Victoria's thinking, she should act the way she does! Learn to recognize your attitude about what she should not do, and then think though it.

Accept what is. You lose your equanimity when you ground it on what "should be." You are being willful to insist that Victoria conform to your way of thinking and acting. It is the accumulation of your own willfulness that gets between God and you, and between others and you.

[Isaiah 55:7-9]

Let God's Love Replace Your Love

Your self-oriented love carried you six years into your marriage, and then it ran out. As you die to the old vision of your marriage, God will give you a new vision. You know how to worship a woman. You know how to be bitter toward a woman. Practice God's love now. Let God's love slowly replace the old broken vision of your marriage.

[Colossians 3:19]

Receive Your Wife's Love

You have tried to draw from Victoria something she cannot give. These attempts brought disappointment and you rejected the love she was able to give. Both of these approaches are wrong. Just as you are to love Victoria as if she were Christ, you also are to receive her love as a gift from God.

Develop space in your relationships. Find Christ's solitude and expression in the relationships. Your marriage and friendships will be more holy as a result.

[Romans 15:7]

Put Sex in Perspective

The overemphasis on sex in our culture has come about in the last forty years or so. Become conscious of how your thinking about the importance and role of sex has been affected by culture and not by Christ.

[Galatians 1:3-5]

Pause, Then Operate from Your Center

You are beginning to identify your "inauthentic" self and how it operates. As you move away from that view, you see the glimmer of the more authentic self. However, so much of the way you do things is based on the old view of yourself.

Operating from your true center, or the more authentic self, is new. Learn to pause before responding when something happens or when someone says something to resurrect old feelings. Your old automatic response may be based on an old fear you have faced and are moving through. Wait and see if a more genuine response to stimulus presents itself. It may surprise you.

[2 Corinthians 5:14-17]

Ride Bigger Horses

You have a habit of walking in a new truth for a while and discarding it when you learn of new truths. Part of this tendency is from your interest in new insights. Do not let new insights hinder your spiritual growth, which comes from walking in truth long enough to make it your own.

Remember your mental image of horses. In it, the horses varied in size, depending on the amount of truth the rider was willing to accept and practice. God wants you to ride bigger and bigger horses. You should not begin with the biggest horse, because you aren't ready for that. On the other hand, don't dismount in favor of smaller horses, either, even if the horses represent new insights.

Consciously dedicate yourself to truth. Write down your challenges and practice truth each day. Summarize the truth so you will read it and do it.

[Psalm 51:6 & 86:11]

Take Off the Press Pass

You like to communicate your ideas in writing as soon as your formulate them. Be careful. If you publish your words about this crisis too soon, you may set back God's work inside you. An oven works best with the door closed.

Be discreet about how and when you tell people what you are going through. Remember, your life will eventually speak out of silence, whether you write or not.

Always examine your motive for publishing. You don't need to publish to boost your self-image, since God already has made you his child. Your attendance before God doesn't depend on your press pass.

[Psalm 46:10]

Epilogue

When the crisis began, my goal was self-confidence in my marriage and at work. Six years later, my confidence has grown, but that is not the most important thing to me anymore. The important thing is that I am more convinced of God's love for me. For that reason, I have become thankful for the crisis.

Thoughts of inadequacy still roll in on occasion like thunder from a receding storm. They rattle old fears and make them seem valid. I remember the truth I have learned and the fears withdraw. These vestiges of insecurity keep me humble and vigilant concerning my recovery. The crisis may have left me with a lifetime of maintenance work.

The crisis left me also with a warmer, less theoretical faith. When I feel insecure, I no longer hide behind my faith. In a way, I embrace my insecurity, knowing that God used it to warm up our relationship. In fact, all the stuff of my twenty-five year Christian walk -- insecurity, sin, repentance, Bible study, prayer -- amounted to precious firewood God and I gathered over the years, waiting for the spark of my crisis to start a comfortable fire for us to share.

I have found my identity in another. And I have moved my soul's furnishings into the abyss and emptiness I feared so much, now that I have found God there.

To Order More Copies

You may order by mail or online at
SlowPress.com.

Mail this form (or the information the
form requests) along with a check payable
to "Slow Press" to the following address:

Slow Press
P. O. Box 92
Bluemont, VA 20135

Title: Dear Me

Number of copies: ___

Name: _____

Address: _____

City, State, Zip: _____

Cost is $7.95 per book, plus shipping.
Shipping is $3.00 for one book and $0.95
per book thereafter.

About the Author

Peter Stephens (shown here with his wife, Victoria) is a pastor of Village Church in Loudoun County, Virginia and a former trial lawyer.

Free Monthly Digest!

Stay up on your slow reading – words that move from our heads to our hearts. Slow Reads Digest is a colorful electronic digest that comes in your email once a month. It contains book reviews, author interviews and other articles at the intersection of reading and meditation.

To sign up or for more information, visit SlowReads.com.